Swimming with Dolphins

By Paul Shipton
Illustrated by Matteo Piana
Activities by Hannah Fish

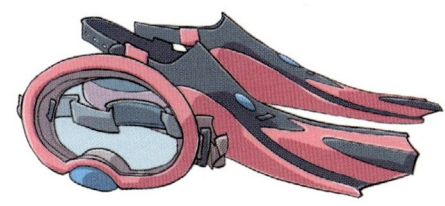

Contents

- Meet the Characters 2
- Swimming with Dolphins 4
- Activities 24
- Project 44
- Picture Dictionary 46
- About Read and Imagine 48
- Key (Activities for Exam Practice) 48

Chapter One

The dolphin jumped high out of the water.

'Wow!' said Rosie. 'Can we swim with it?'

'No, I'm sorry,' said Dan Miller, a scientist who worked with the dolphins. Grandpa, Ben, Rosie, and Alice were visiting Dan. Years ago, he was one of Grandpa's students.

'All our dolphins have had injuries,' Dan explained. 'We help them to go out to the sea again when they are ready.'

'Before we send a dolphin out to sea, we put a small radio on its fin,' explained Dan. 'Then we can follow it on the computer. Come and see.'

Grandpa and the children went with Dan into an office.

In the office a scientist was sitting in front of a computer. She turned in her chair and said, 'Dan, come and look at this. There's a problem with Ludo.'

'Who's Ludo?' asked Alice.

'Ludo is a young dolphin that we looked after for a long time,' said Dan. 'We sent him back to the sea a few days ago.'

He looked at the computer unhappily.

'What's the problem?' asked Grandpa.

'Ludo has been under the water for twenty minutes,' said Dan. 'He isn't moving.'

'Can't dolphins stay under the water for a long time?' asked Ben.

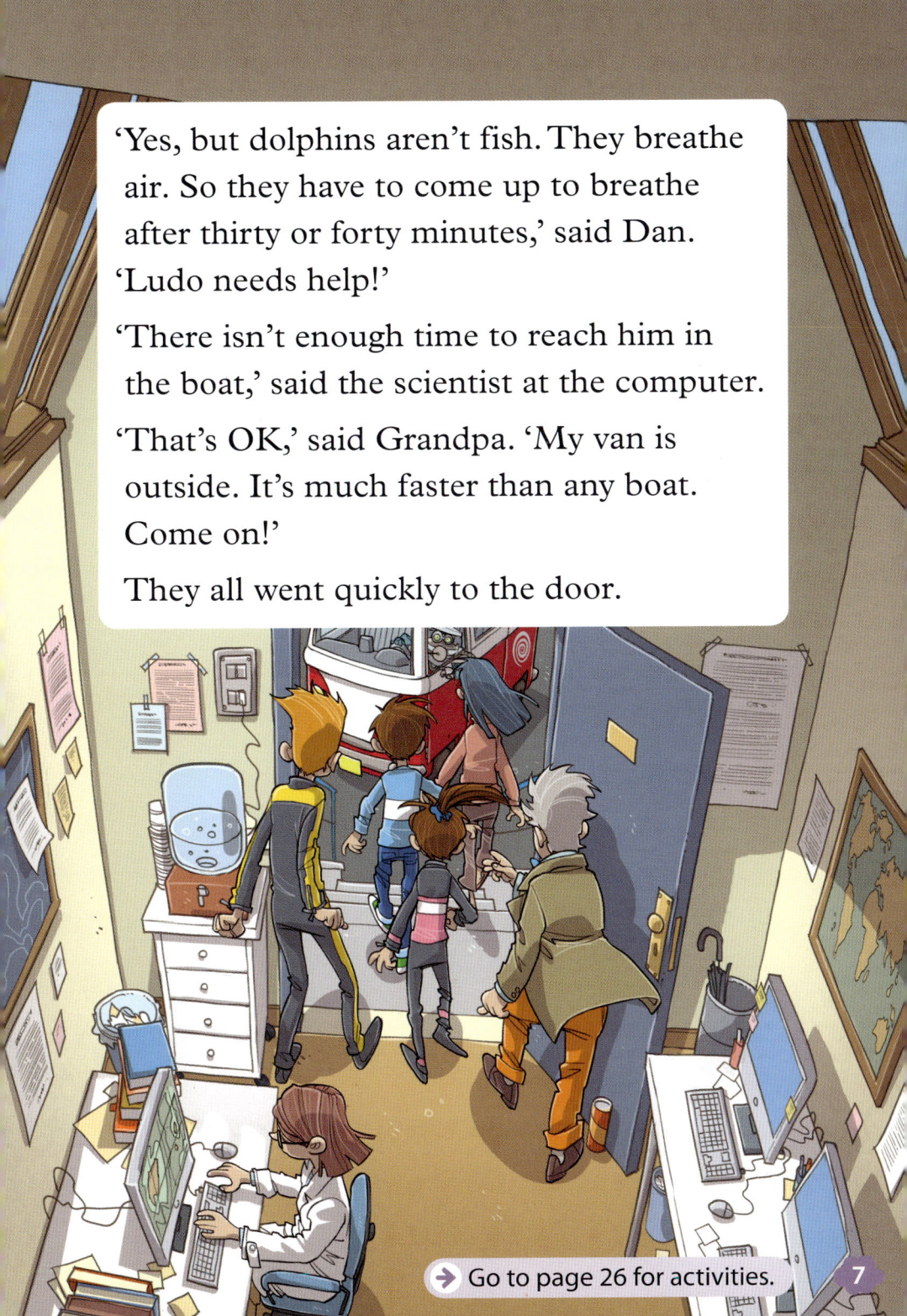

'Yes, but dolphins aren't fish. They breathe air. So they have to come up to breathe after thirty or forty minutes,' said Dan. 'Ludo needs help!'

'There isn't enough time to reach him in the boat,' said the scientist at the computer.

'That's OK,' said Grandpa. 'My van is outside. It's much faster than any boat. Come on!'

They all went quickly to the door.

Go to page 26 for activities.

Chapter Two

While Clunk drove, Dan got his diving equipment ready.

'Ludo was a little afraid so he stayed close to the shore,' Dan explained. 'Perhaps he can't move because of a fishing line.' He looked at his watch. 'When will we arrive there?'

'We're there now!' said Clunk. The children looked out the window at the blue sky all around them.

'Please land on the water,' Grandpa told the robot.

But there was a problem. The sea here wasn't very deep, and Clunk didn't see the rocks under the water.

CRASH! There was a terrible sound as the van hit one of the rocks.

'Water is coming into the van!' shouted Ben.

Grandpa jumped up. 'Clunk, get the tools, please,' he said. 'We have to fix this quickly.'

While Grandpa tried to fix the van, Clunk used a bucket to throw out the water.

→ Go to page 28 for activities.

'While we're doing this, you can dive into the water and help the dolphin, Dan,' said Grandpa.

But Dan didn't answer.

'He hit his head when the van hit the rock,' said Ben.

Rosie jumped up.

'What are you doing?' Ben asked.

His little sister was putting on some diving equipment. 'I'm the best swimmer and I know how to dive,' Rosie said quickly.

'Rosie, wait …' began Alice.

'Ludo needs our help NOW,' said Rosie. Ben, can you look after Dan? I'm going to help Ludo.'

She put the diving mask over her face and jumped into the water.

Ben was sitting with Dan. The scientist opened his eyes and put one hand to his head.

'What happened?' he asked. Then he looked around. 'Why is there water inside the van? And where's Rosie?'

→ Go to page 30 for activities.

Chapter Three

Ben tried to explain. 'Rosie dived into the water to help Ludo,' he said. 'He needs help quickly.'

Dan looked very afraid. 'I've dived here often,' he said. 'It can be very dangerous.'

'Why?' asked Alice.

'There are sharks here,' said Dan.

For the first time, Grandpa looked up from his work.

In the water, Rosie was swimming down.

She was a strong swimmer and she loved being in the sea. But this time she did not stop to look at any of the fish as they swam past her.

She saw a large shape close to the sea floor.

It was Ludo! The dolphin was moving his tail up and down, but he could not swim away.

→ Go to page 32 for activities.

When she was close enough, Rosie saw the problem. There was an old fishing line around Ludo's body. One end of the line was around a rock on the sea floor.

Rosie tried to break the fishing line, but it was too strong. Carefully she started to take the fishing line off the dolphin. Ludo stopped kicking his tail.

'He understands,' thought Rosie. 'He's trying to help me!'

At last, Rosie pulled away the fishing line. Ludo could swim again!

Rosie watched happily as the dolphin kicked his tail and swam up to get some air.

Rosie began to swim up, too.

Then she saw a large shape in the water. 'What's Ludo doing now?' she thought.

But the shape wasn't Ludo.

It wasn't a dolphin.

It was a shark …

Chapter Four

On the van, Dan was looking for more diving equipment.

'Can we take the van under the water?' asked Alice.

'Not until I fix it,' said Grandpa.

Ben was watching the water nervously. Suddenly a head came up out of the water.

'There's Rosie!' Ben shouted.

Rosie started to swim to the van.

'What's that in the water behind her?' asked Alice.

'Is it Ludo?' asked Ben.

'No,' said Dan. 'That's a shark's fin! A big one!'

'Rosie!' shouted Ben. 'Swim faster!'

Rosie swam as fast as she could. But she couldn't swim faster than a shark, and she knew it. The shark was coming closer and closer.

Dan got ready to jump in. He had to help Rosie. But how?

He didn't know, but he had to try.

Before Dan dived in, a gray head came up out of the water next to Rosie. It was Ludo! The dolphin was here to help her.

Rosie put both of her hands around the dolphin's fin. 'Go!' she shouted.

Ludo kicked his tail and started swimming to the van. It wasn't easy, but Rosie held onto the fin.

'Swim, Ludo!' shouted Dan. 'You can do it!'

Ben turned and said, 'Grandpa, can we move the van closer? Is it ready yet?'

Grandpa was too busy to look up. 'In one minute,' he answered.

But did Rosie have one minute? The shark could swim faster than Ludo. It was behind Rosie and the dolphin, and it was coming closer and closer.

Chapter Five

Suddenly Ludo dived under the water. Rosie tried to hold onto his fin, but she couldn't. She saw another gray shape in the water. Was it the shark? More gray shapes swam past her. What was happening?

Four or five new dolphins were here! One swam and hit the shark with its nose. Then another dolphin did the same thing.

In the van, Dan was watching it all. 'The shark is swimming away!' he said.

Clunk helped Rosie to get out of the water.

'Rosie, we were very frightened!' said Alice.

'I was frightened too,' said Rosie. 'But Ludo and the other dolphins were fantastic!'

Go to page 40 for activities.

'What's that in your hand, Rosie?' asked Alice.

Rosie looked down. 'It's the radio that was on Ludo's fin,' she said. She turned to Dan. 'I'm sorry. It broke when Ludo was pulling me in the water.'

'That's OK,' said Dan. He pointed to Ludo, who was swimming close to the van.

'He's smiling!' said Ben.

The children could see the other dolphins in the water too.

'I was following Ludo with the radio because he hasn't lived in the sea for a long time,' said Dan. 'He didn't have any friends.' Dan smiled. 'But he has friends now.'

Ludo came up high out of the water.

'He's saying goodbye,' said Alice.

'Goodbye, Ludo,' said Dan.

They watched as Ludo and his new dolphin friends turned and swam out together to deeper water.

Go to page 42 for activities.

Activities for pages 4–5

1 Choose and write the correct words.

> a fin   scientists   an injury   ~~an office~~
> students   a dolphin   a computer

1 This is a place where people work.   _an office_
2 These people work in science.   _____
3 This is an animal that lives in water.   _____
4 You can find this on a dolphin.   _____
5 This is when something has hurt a person or animal's body.   _____

2 Order the words.

1 to swim / Rosie / the dolphin. / wanted / with
   Rosie wanted to swim with the dolphin.

2 with / is / Dan / a scientist / dolphins. / who works
   _____

3 had / the dolphins / injuries. / have / All
   _____

4 put / on / a radio / They / fins. / the dolphins'
   _____

5 the computer. / they can / the dolphins / follow / Then / on
   _____

3 Circle the correct words.

1 The dolphin jumped out **to** / **of** the water.
2 **Can** / **Are** we swim with it?
3 They can't **swimming** / **swim** with the dolphin.
4 Grandpa and the children were **visiting** / **visit** Dan.
5 Dan was one **off** / **of** Grandpa's students.
6 Dan helps **they** / **them** to go out to sea again.
7 They **put** / **puts** a radio on the dolphins' fins.

4 Match. Then write the sentences.

1 Grandpa and the children — went with Dan into an office.
2 There was — a problem with Ludo.
3 A scientist was — sitting in front of a computer.
4 The scientist — turned in her chair.

1 Grandpa and the children went with Dan into an office.
2 _____
3 _____
4 _____

Talk Do you like dolphins? Would you like to swim with dolphins? Talk to a friend.

Activities for pages 6–7

1 Complete the sentences.

> sent   breathe   ~~looked~~   stay   ran   needs

1 The scientists __looked__ after Ludo for a long time.
2 They _____ Ludo back to sea a few days ago.
3 Dolphins can _____ under the water for a long time.
4 Dolphins aren't fish. They _____ air.
5 'Ludo _____ help!'
6 They all _____ to the door.

2 Look at the picture on page 7 and write *yes* or *no*.

1 Clunk is in the van.   __yes__
2 Dan is using a computer.   _____
3 You can see a dolphin.   _____
4 There's a map in the office.   _____
5 Ben is in the van.   _____
6 The scientist at the computer has a white coat.   _____

Talk Can they help Ludo? Tell a friend your ideas.

3 Choose and write the correct words.

Grandpa and the children were visiting a ¹ _scientist_ called Dan Miller. Dan helps dolphins with injuries. When the dolphins are ready, Dan sends them out to ² _____. They sent a dolphin called Ludo out to sea a few days ago. Ludo has a ³ _____ on his fin. Now there is a problem. Dolphins ⁴ _____ air. Ludo is under the water. He needs help to come up to the ⁵ _____.

| dolphin | radio | air | sea |

| ~~scientist~~ | water | injury | breathe |

Now tick (✓) the best name for Chapter One.

Ludo needs water! ☐
Ludo needs fish! ☐
Ludo needs help! ☐

Activities for pages 8–9

1 Write the words.

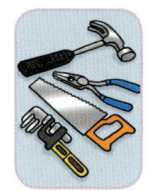  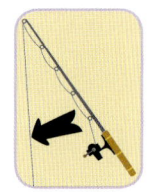

1 __tools__ 2 _____ 3 _____

 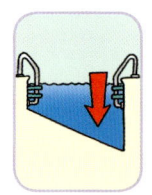 

4 _____ 5 _____ 6 _____

2 Look at pages 8 and 9 and complete the sentences. You can use 1, 2, 3, or 4 words.

1 Ludo was afraid so he stayed close __to the shore__ .
2 The children looked _____ window.
3 Clunk _____ the rocks under the water.
4 The van hit _____ rocks.
5 Water was coming _____ the van.
6 Grandpa tried _____ van.
7 Clunk _____ to throw out the water.

3 Choose the best answers.

1 Clunk: Where do you want me to land the van?
   Grandpa: __c__

2 Clunk: What was that sound?
   Grandpa: ____

3 Clunk: Is the van broken?
   Grandpa: ____

4 Clunk: How can we fix it?
   Grandpa: ____

5 Clunk: Do you want me to get the tools?
   Grandpa: ____

> a We need the tools.
>
> b We need to help him.
>
> ~~c~~ On the water.
>
> d Yes, we are!
>
> e Yes, please.
>
> f The van hit a rock!
>
> g Yes, it is!

 for pages 10-11

1 Write *yes* or *no*.

1 Dan hit his head. ___yes___
2 Ben put on some diving equipment. _____
3 Rosie doesn't know how to dive. _____
4 Rosie jumped into the water. _____
5 Ben was sitting with Dan. _____
6 Dan didn't open his eyes. _____

2 Answer the questions.

1 What happened to Dan?
   He hit his head when the van hit the rock.
2 What did Rosie put on?
   _____
3 Who is the best swimmer?
   _____
4 Why does Ludo need help now?
   _____
5 Why did Rosie jump into the water?
   _____

Talk Can Rosie help Ludo? Tell a friend your ideas.

3 Choose and write the correct words.

Dan didn't ¹ ___answer___ Grandpa. He hit
² _____ head when the van hit the rock.
Rosie put ³ _____ some diving equipment.
Rosie is a good swimmer and she can dive. Rosie
put the mask ⁴ _____ her face and jumped
into the water. Dan ⁵ _____ his eyes. 'What
happened?' he asked.

1 ~~answer~~ answering answers

2 him he's his

3 off in on

4 over at above

5 open opening opened

4 Write the words from Chapter Two.

1 r a h c s   ___crash___
2 h o t r w u t o   _____ _____
3 u t p n o   _____ _____
4 e d i v   _____
5 v g i d i n k s a m   _____ _____
6 i s t i n c e s t   _____

Activities for pages 12–13

1 Choose and write the correct words.

a swimmer   a diving mask   dive

shapes   a shark   ~~a tail~~

1 You can find this on many animals.   <u> a tail </u>

2 This is a person that swims.   _____

3 This animal lives in the sea.   _____

4 This is when you swim down under
   the water.   _____

5 Circles and squares are these.   _____

2 Look at the picture on page 13 and write *yes* or *no*.

1 Rosie is wearing diving equipment.   _____

2 Ludo is yellow.   _____

3 There are some fish in the water.   _____

3 Circle the mistakes. Then write the correct words.

1 Rosie dived (on) the water to help Ludo. ___into___
2 It can been very dangerous here. _____
3 There is sharks here. _____
4 Rosie was a strongest swimmer. _____
5 Ludo was move his tail up and down. _____
6 Ludo could no swim away. _____

4 Match. Then write the sentences.

It can be dangerous	but he couldn't swim away.
Rosie loved	because there are sharks.
Rosie could see	being in the sea.
Ludo was moving,	a shape close to the sea floor.

1 _____
2 _____
3 _____
4 _____

Talk What has happened to Ludo? Tell a friend your ideas.

Activities for pages 14–15

1 Write the words from Chapter Three.

1 e a s   o o l f r   _____ _____
2 c o k r   _____
3 t r s n o g   _____
4 u r e n d s t n a d   _____
5 h a s p e   _____
6 i s f h n i g   i n l e   _____ _____

2 Answer the questions.

1 What was the problem with Ludo?
_____

2 How did Rosie help Ludo?
_____

3 Where did Ludo swim?
_____

4 What did Rosie see in the water?
_____

5 What was the shape?
_____

Talk Are you scared of sharks? Talk to a friend.
What does Rosie do? Tell a friend your ideas.

3 Order the events in Chapter Three.

Dan tells Ben about the sharks. _____
Rosie sees Ludo close to the sea floor. _____
Rosie pulls the fishing line away from Ludo. _____
Rosie dives into the water to help Ludo. __1__
Ludo stops kicking his tail to help Rosie. _____
Rosie sees a shark in the water. _____

4 Choose and write the correct words.

Rosie ¹ _____ into the water to help Ludo. Ludo could not swim away. He had a fishing line around his body. Rosie ² _____ the fishing line away from Ludo. He swam up to get some ³ _____. Then Rosie saw a shape in the water. It was a ⁴ _____!

| pulled | shapes | shark | dived | air |

Now tick (✓) the best name for Chapter Three.

Rosie helps Ludo ☐   Rosie pulls Ludo ☐
Ludo moves his tail ☐

# Activities for pages 16–17

1 Complete the sentences.

> coming   fixing   ~~looking~~
> getting   shouting   watching

1 Dan was ___looking___ for more diving equipment.
2 Grandpa was _____ the van.
3 Ben was _____ the water nervously.
4 Ben was _____ to Rosie.
5 The shark was _____ closer and closer.
6 Dan was _____ ready to jump in.

2 Who said this? Write the names.

1 'Rosie! Swim faster!' _____
2 'Can we take the van under the water?' _____
3 'Not until I fix it.' _____
4 'That's a shark's fin! A big one!' _____
5 'There's Rosie!' _____
6 'What's that in the water behind her?' _____
7 'Is it Ludo?' _____

3 Choose the best answers.

1 Dan: Where is Rosie?
   Ben: ____
2 Dan: What is she doing?
   Ben: ____
3 Dan: What is that behind her?
   Ben: ____
4 Dan: I don't know. But I can try.
   Ben: ____
5 Dan: I'm not sure. Can you help me?
   Ben: ____

a It's a shark. Can you help her?

b It's the van.

c She's trying to help Ludo.

d She's in the water.

e What are you going to do?

f What is she going to do?

g Yes, I'll do everything I can to help.

Activities for pages 18–19

1 Circle the correct words.

1 Ludo came to **fix** / **help** Rosie.
2 Rosie put her hands around the dolphin's **head** / **fin**.
3 Ludo started swimming to the **van** / **shore**.
4 Grandpa was **driving** / **fixing** the van.
5 The shark **couldn't** / **could** swim faster than Ludo.
6 The shark was **behind** / **in front** of Ludo and Rosie.

2 Order the words.

1 gray head / up / A / out of / came / the water.
　_____

2 kicked / started / Ludo / his tail / and / swimming.
　_____

3 easy, but / held onto / It / the fin. / Rosie / wasn't
　_____

4 the van / Can / move / closer? / we
　_____

5 was / to / Grandpa / too busy / up. / look
　_____

Talk Can Ludo and Rosie get to the van? Tell a friend your ideas.

3 Choose and write the correct words.

Rosie was swimming to [1] _____ van. But the shark was behind her. Suddenly Ludo came [2] _____ help her. Rosie held onto [3] _____ fin. Grandpa was fixing the van, but [4] _____ wasn't ready yet. The dolphin was swimming to the van. But the shark could swim faster, [5] _____ it was coming closer and closer.

| 1 that the a |
| 2 for to and |
| 3 Ludos Ludo Ludo's |

| 4 it that this |
| 5 then but and |

4 Order the events in Chapter Four.

Rosie starts to swim to the van. ____
Ludo comes to help Rosie. ____
Ben is watching the water nervously. ____
Ludo starts to swim to the van with Rosie. ____
Dan sees a shark's fin behind Rosie. ____
Rosie put her hands around Ludo's fin. ____

 **Activities** for pages 20–21

1 Write *yes* or *no*.

1 When Ludo dived, Rosie couldn't hold his fin. _____

2 Rosie saw a lot of gray shapes in the water. _____

3 The dolphins started to hit the shark with their fins. _____

4 The shark swam away. _____

5 Ben helped Rosie to get out of the water. _____

6 Rosie wasn't frightened. _____

2 Circle the mistakes. Then write the correct words.

1 Suddenly Ludo dived out of the water again. _____

2 Rosie tried for hold Ludo's fin. _____

3 Gray shapes swimming past Rosie. _____

4 A dolphin hit the shark with the nose. _____

5 Behind the van, Dan was watching. _____

6 Clunk helped Rosie to get up of the water. _____

7 The dolphins was fantastic! _____

3 Look at pages 20 and 21 and complete the sentences. You can use 1, 2, 3, or 4 words.

1 Rosie tried _____ Ludo's fin, but she couldn't.
2 Rosie saw another _____ water.
3 Four or _____ were here!
4 One dolphin hit _____ with its nose.
5 In the van, Dan _____ all.
6 Ludo and _____ were fantastic!

4 What is it?

1 It's a ___nose___ .   2 It's a _____ .

3 It's a _____ .   4 It's a _____ .

Activities for pages 22–23

1 Write the words.

close   smile   radio   point   hand   break

   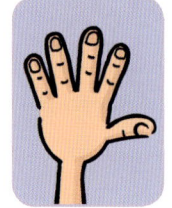   

1 _____   2 _____   3 _____

4 _____   5 _____   6 _____

2 Who said this? Write the names.

1 'He's smiling!' _____

2 'Goodbye, Ludo.' _____

3 'What's that in your hand, Rosie?' _____

4 'He didn't have any friends. But he has friends now.' _____

5 'It's the radio that was on Ludo's fin.' _____

6 'He's saying goodbye.' _____

3 Choose and write the correct words.

Four or five new dolphins were here. They [1] _____ the shark with their noses. The shark swam away. Clunk [2] _____ Rosie to get out of the water. The [3] _____ could see the other dolphins. Now Ludo had some friends. Ludo came up high out of the [4] _____ to say goodbye. Then Ludo and his friends swam out to [5] _____ water.

water   dived   deeper   swam

hit   shark   helped   children

Now tick (✓) the best name for Chapter Five.

Ludo and the children ☐
Ludo and his friends ☐
Clunk helps Rosie ☐

Talk **Do you like this story? Talk to a friend.**

Project
Dolphin and Shark Research

1 Do some research on dolphins and try to answer all the questions.

How many kinds of dolphin are there?

What kind of dolphin is the largest?

What color are most dolphins?

What do dolphins eat?

Do they live in groups?

How do they talk to each other?

How deep can they swim?

How do they breathe?

How long can they stay under the water?

What problems do they have?

2 Now do some research on sharks and try to answer all the questions.

How many kinds of shark are there?

What kind of shark is the largest?

What color are most sharks?

What do sharks eat?

How many teeth do they have?

Do they live in groups?

How deep can they swim?

How do they breathe?

How many babies do they have?

Why are they dangerous?

Talk Do you prefer dolphins or sharks? Why? Talk to a friend.

Picture Dictionary

 boat

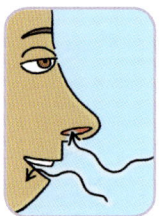 breathe

 bucket

 crash

 dangerous

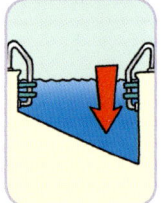 deep

 dive

 diving equipment

 diving mask

 dolphin

 fin

 fish

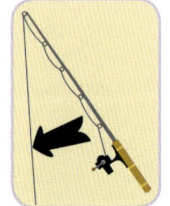 fishing line

 fix

 hold onto

 injury

land	nervous	office	put on (*past* put on)

radio	rock	scientist	sea

shark	shore	smile	swim

tail	throw	tools	water

Oxford Read and Imagine

Oxford Read and Imagine graded readers are at eight levels (Starter, Beginner, and Levels 1 to 6) for students from age 4 and older. They offer great stories to read and enjoy.

Activities provide Cambridge Young Learner Exams preparation. See Key below.

At Levels 1 to 6, every storybook reader links to an **Oxford Read and Discover** non-fiction reader, giving students a chance to find out more about the world around them, and an opportunity for Content and Language Integrated Learning (CLIL).

For more information about **Read and Imagine**, and for Teacher's Notes, go to www.oup.com/elt/teacher/readandimagine

KEY
 Activity supports Cambridge Young Learners Movers Exam preparation
 Activity supports Cambridge Young Learners Flyers Exam preparation

Oxford Read and Discover

Do you want to find out more about dolphins, sharks, and how animals eat and live in the sea? You can read this non-fiction book.

OXFORD
UNIVERSITY PRESS

Great Clarendon Street, Oxford, OX2 6DP, United Kingdom

Oxford University Press is a department of the University of Oxford. It furthers the University's objective of excellence in research, scholarship, and education by publishing worldwide. Oxford is a registered trade mark of Oxford University Press in the UK and in certain other countries

© Oxford University Press 2014

The moral rights of the author have been asserted

First published in 2014

2018 2017 2016 2015 2014

10 9 8 7 6 5 4 3 2 1

No unauthorized photocopying

All rights reserved. No part of this publication may be reproduced, stored in a retrieval system, or transmitted, in any form or by any means, without the prior permission in writing of Oxford University Press, or as expressly permitted by law, by licence or under terms agreed with the appropriate reprographics rights organization.

Enquiries concerning reproduction outside the scope of the above should be sent to the ELT Rights Department, Oxford University Press, at the address above

You must not circulate this work in any other form and you must impose this same condition on any acquirer

Links to third party websites are provided by Oxford in good faith and for information only. Oxford disclaims any responsibility for the materials contained in any third party website referenced in this work

ISBN: 978 0 19 472361 9

Printed in China

This book is printed on paper from certified and well-managed sources

ACKNOWLEDGEMENTS

Main illustrations by: Matteo Piana.

Additional illustrations by: Dusan Pavlic/Beehive Illustration, Alan Rowe, Mark Ruffle.